W9-BKR-063

Making Social Studies
COME ALIVE

65 Teacher-Tested Ideas for Classroom Use

By
Marilyn Kretzer
Marlene Slobin
Madella Williams

SCHOLASTIC
PROFESSIONAL BOOKS

New York • Toronto • London • Auckland • Sydney

FRANKLIN PIERCE
COLLEGE LIBRARY
RINDGE, N.H. 03461

Acknowledgments

To our students, who inspired us to go "beyond the textbook" with new and fresh perspectives. To our friends, throughout our districts, who gave us their support and ideas. To our principals, Mike Leach and Joe Nuber. They have encouraged us to grow as teachers and bring recognition to our schools, and they allowed us the time to share our expertise.

And finally, our special thanks to our families, who provide us with our greatest inspiration, encourage us to share our love of teaching and students with others, and take pride in all that we do:

Frank, Seth, and Jessica Kretzer
Lester, Scott, and Todd Slobin
Lewis and Devota Williams

Scholastic Inc. grants teachers permission to photocopy the reproducible pages from this book for classroom use. No other part of this publication may be reproduced in whole or in part, or stored in a retrieval system, or transmitted in any form or by any means, electronic, mechanical, photocopying, recording, or otherwise, without permission of the publisher. For information regarding permission, write to:
Scholastic Professional Books, 555 Broadway, New York, NY 10012-3999.

Interior design by Carmen Robert Sorvillo
Cover design by Vincent Ceci and Jaime Lucero
Cover photo by Childs/Muniz
Photographs by Marlene Slobin

ISBN 0-590-96381-3

Copyright © 1996 Marilyn Kretzer, Marlene Slobin, and Madella Williams. All rights reserved.

Printed in the U.S.A.
12 11 10 9 8 7 6 5 4 3 2 1 4 5/9

CURR
LB
1584
.K67
1996

Table of Contents

Section One:
Geography

Map-Making Activities

Map Skills Activities

Other Geography Activities

Section Two:
History

Timeline Activities

Researching and Reporting: People of the Past

Focusing on Events and Ideas

Section Three:
Culture

Art Activities

Food Activities

Holiday Activities

Introduction

A number of years ago, we listened to a variety of presentations while attending a state social studies convention. The presentations were interesting, but uninspiring; they did not provide us with new ideas on how to involve students in their own learning, or on how to help them develop higher level thinking skills. We took it as our personal goal to create a session for the next year's meeting which would help provide teachers with more stimulating, motivating activities for their social studies students.

Although we teach different grade levels and subjects, we discovered that we shared (and still do) a similar philosophy about hands-on learning situations for our students. We also realized that our teaching methods were similar and our ideas could easily be adapted to various grade levels, subject matter, and learning styles.

Because they are usually presented with textbooks and given the standard assignments, students tend to perceive social studies classes as boring. All too often teachers give assignments consisting of "read the chapter, make an outline and then answer the questions at the end." This may be because teachers do not know how to approach or do not yet feel comfortable with alternative forms of assessment. Additionally, we are all fighting the "Boring Battle," as in "this class is boring...," "life is boring...," "school is boring...," "history is boring." Students perceive history teachers as "old," having had to live all the history themselves before they could possibly teach it! We accepted these statements as our greatest challenge.

Our aim is to share our creative teaching styles and activities to help other teachers stimulate, motivate, and challenge their students. Teachers who constantly try new ideas and incorporate a variety of hands-on-activities into their lessons feel refreshed even after many years in the classroom. Teachers continually borrow ideas from one another, adapting and changing them as we have done over the years. Some of our activities may be new to you, or some may be ones you already use in your classrooms, but perhaps with a different spin or slant to them. Hopefully, we have given you new ways to approach some things you've done the same way for years. Our collaboration has taken us throughout our state, to various school districts, and across the country. We hope that teachers and ultimately their students have been enriched through some of our activities. We certainly have been enriched by sharing our ideas with hundreds of other teachers and hope to continue to be. We hope that our strategies and activities will continue to help other teachers prove that social studies is alive and well, and living in their classrooms.

Alternative Assessment:
Making It Work for You and Your Students

Teachers who have stayed away from alternative assessment projects because they felt uncomfortable in grading them may find that a rubric makes assessment much easier for themselves and their students. Create a rubric with the students for each project. (See *Examples Of Rubrics* on page 7.) Students need to understand the various parts of a project as well as the evaluation process which will be used. If students participate in making the rubric, they will feel more a part of the procedure. Students will remember material that you have taught them if they can work with it in a variety of ways in addition to paper and pencil tests. The following is a list of suggestions on how to make alternative assessment an integral part of your classroom.

- Vary your activities to address all the different learning styles in the classroom. Grades and self-esteem will improve.

- Give students choices of activities and working arrangements.

- Each time you do an activity in class, make notes on what worked, what didn't, and how to improve and modify the lesson. Never give up on a good activity, even if it bombs in one class. Adjust and move on.

- Never take an activity directly from a book or fellow teacher without adapting or modifying it to your teaching style and your students' learning styles. Every teacher and every class is different. Make the activity your own!

- Model creativity. You can't tell students to be creative as you stand in a sterile environment, or use lecture as your sole teaching method.

- Decorate your classroom. By displaying student work, you are sending students the message that you value what they have done.

- Explanation of the activity is as important as the activity itself. Make sure all students understand the directions, as well as why they are doing this activity.

- Worksheets are sometimes necessary. Make them more appealing by adding a decorative border or cartoon.

- Show enthusiasm. Students have a sixth sense and know when you, the teacher, like what you are doing. If the teacher is apathetic about a lesson, the students will be as well.

- There is no way that you can change every lesson you do all at once. Change a lesson gradually and before you know it, you'll have an extensive collection of activities.

- Keep examples of good projects from year to year to show as models. Your visual learners will turn in much better work if they have an image or idea of a finished product.

- If possible, videotape your students as they present their projects. The ideal situation is for each student have a personal tape, recording everything done in class. This visual portfolio provides students with a collection of their work. Often when students see themselves on tape, they recognize distracting mannerisms such as playing with hair, rocking back and forth, etc. Most often, by the end of the year, students make the correction themselves.

- Stretch your personality. Come dressed as a historical figure from the time period you are studying. Have some fun!

Examples of Rubrics

Creating a rubric is very important. The rubric will set the standards for the project. It needs to be specific enough to produce effortless interpretation for scoring purposes. It is very important that the students see and understand the rubric before the task. The criteria for evaluation (the rubric) should be given to students prior to their starting the project. For best results, make a rubric with the students. If they have a part in creating the rubric, they will have a better understanding of the scoring and the project.

Make the rubric easy on yourself. Select four or five categories and award points depending on the number of divisions. For example, for five categories, the point division for each might be:

Excellent: . . . . . 25-23 points
Good: . . . . 22-20 points
Fair: . . . . 19-18 points
Poor: . . . . 17-16 points
No credit: 0

When making the rubric, be clear about what you want the students to accomplish. Hopefully, the information that follows will be helpful.

Requirements:

4 Points - All requirements present.
3 Points - For the most part requirements are present.
2 Points - Some requirements are present but with some mistakes.
1 Point - Missing or disconnected requirements.

Comprehension of basic content and concepts:

4 Points - Demonstrates a complete comprehension of the basic content and concepts.
3 Points - Demonstrates a competent comprehension of basic content and concepts; minor errors, but not a distraction from the overall response.
2 Points - Demonstrates a marginal comprehension of basic content and concepts; major errors of fact are present.
1 Point - Demonstrates little comprehension.

Correctness:

4 Points - Completely correct.
3 Points - Correct for the most part; minor errors.
2 Points - Partially correct; major errors.
1 Point - Incorrect.

About this Book

This book is divided into three sections: geography, history, and culture. Each section contains a variety of activities for individual, group, and class use. In addition to objectives and a list of needed materials, you'll find suggestions for expanding many of the activities into larger projects.

Section One
GEOGRAPHY

Geography is usually not on students' lists of favorite subjects, probably because it so frequently is limited to matching states and capitals, countries and capitals, or labeling rivers and oceans on a map. We've discovered that geography can be fun for students when it focuses on their current interests.

Map-Making Activities

Encourage students to become amateur cartographers by providing hands-on map-making activities. The purpose of these activities is for students to construct a map without the use of paper and pencil. These activities will help your students expand their perspectives of location and develop vocabulary for geography.

 **Yarning Around**

◢ Objectives
- Locate and explain the importance of various places
- Use problem-solving skills

◢ Materials
- Yarn - approximately 18-24 inches for each student
- Small pieces of paper for labeling places on the map
- Atlas

Organize students into small groups. Give each student a piece of yarn. (The amount of yarn depends on what you want the students to create.) Tell them that they are cartographers, and they will attempt to shape continents, countries, or states on their desk tops. Give the various groups small pieces of paper and have the students identify borders, landforms, and bodies of water, write them on paper slips, and then place them in the correct location on their maps. Students should then consult an atlas to check the accuracy of their work.

 **Lands of Imagination**

◢ Objective
- Create an original map

Using students' geography skills, have them create a map of an imaginary area based on their own interests, for example, Hamburger Land, Ice Cream Land, Heart Land. Each map should include a compass rose, a key, map symbols, and names of important sites.

Junior Cartographer

🔺 **Objective** • Locate and identify neighborhood landmarks

🔺 **Materials** • String

Have students write the words: home, school, library, hospital, police station, fire station, friend's house, or other neighborhood places on separate, small pieces of paper. Then invite students to use string to create a simple map of their community, correctly placing the neighborhood landmarks on the map. You might want to ask how many students placed their home in the middle of the map. The students will feel like real cartographers when you explain that this was a common practice used by the first known cartographers, who drew the world in relation to their own countries.

Bag Your State

🔺 **Objective** • Locate major cities and landforms

🔺 **Materials**
• Orange or yellow yarn long enough to make an outline of your state
• Blue yarn cut in pieces for the number of rivers in your state. (You can change yarn color except for the rivers.)
• Index cards labeled with major cities, rivers, lakes, or other landforms
• Paper or plastic bags

In a paper bag, place enough yellow or orange yarn to make an outline of your state. Also include blue yarn of various lengths for rivers. (The amounts and colors of yarn depend on the state that you are doing.) On index cards, label the names of the major cities, rivers, and other landforms. Make a master of the labels and duplicate the master, then all you need do is cut up the labels.

12

Organize students in small groups and give each group a bag with the yarn and labels. Have each group form an outline of your state with the yellow or brown yarn, without consulting a map. Tell students to place the blue string where they think the major rivers are located. After they have completed their "yarn drawing," ask students to place the names of the cities and landforms in their correct locations. When students have completed this part of the activity, have them consult a map to check their accuracy. "Bag Your State" is a good way to test students' knowledge at the beginning of the year and again at the end.

Teacher Tips

If your state has more than two geographical areas, give the groups 25-inch strands of yarn (the number depends on how many geographical regions are in your state). Have students divide their yarn map into regions. Students can create and place symbols for the products and natural resources of each region in the proper place.

5 Home Sweet Home

 **Objective**
- Draw a map of a familiar place
- Trace a route on a map

Have students create a map from home to school. (This lesson should come at the point when students are familiar with map symbols and directions.) A fun motivator is to tell students that they have won a contest. However, the only way their cash and prizes can be delivered is if they provide a clear and accurate map to their house. Students are to create a map showing the route from their home to their school. Maps must be neat, easy to read, and contain proper map symbols with a key and compass rose. This is a good "at home" project, but allow at least one weekend in case students need a parent to drive them to help clock the distance. You might want to reward students with some type of "prize."

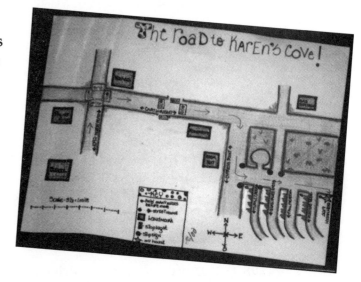

Map Skills Activities

These activities provide opportunities for practicing map skills and expose students to the different kinds of information that maps can show.

6 Follow Your Team

Objective
- Identify and locate cities on a map

Materials
- United States map
- *Sports Teams* reproducible (page 24)
- Itinerary for a sports team

Obtain a copy of a major sports team's itinerary for the season. If possible, choose a team located in your city or state or one that students follow. Have students locate and mark on a map the cities to which the team travels for out-of-town games. This can be done in small groups or as a class activity, depending on the age of your students.

Teacher Tips

You might also have students research and discuss how and why various teams got their names; for example, the Pittsburgh Steelers, Phoenix Suns, Portland Trailblazers.

7 Hoop It Up!

Objective
- Use geographical, cultural, or historical clues to identify sports teams
- Locate cities on a map

Materials
- United States map

This is a more advanced activity and one that will provide older students with a chance to show off their sports knowledge as well as geography skills. Organize students into groups and give them a list of sports teams. The list should include only the nickname of the team, for example: *Dolphins*. The students have to first figure out what city the team is from, and then locate the city on a map. As an additional challenge, have students explain how the team name relates to the geography, culture, or history of its hometown.

Teacher Tips

If your community is not already home to a major league team, ask students to imagine that it soon will be. Have students think of appropriate names for the team based on geographical, cultural, or historical information. Students might also pick other cities without major league teams and determine team names for them as well.

8 Team Pictures

◔ **Objective**
- Identify and locate cities on a map

◬ **Materials**
- United States map
- Pictures of members of major league football teams

Divide the class into two groups: the National Football League National Conference and the National Football League American Conference (you can further divide these into Eastern, Central, and Western divisions). Have students collect pictures of players from the teams and place these pictures on a map at cities that correspond to each player's home team.

9 Rock around the Country!

◔ **Objective**
- Plan an itinerary

◬ **Materials**
- United States map
- Blank U.S. (outline) maps

This is a multi-purpose geography activity. It can be used when studying the world, the United States, or your own state. Students make an itinerary for a favorite musical group, real or imaginary. Groups can be rock-and-roll, rap, country, classical, or alternative. Students should take into consideration location, population, accessible sites, and a variety of factors that would make for a successful concert tour.

Before beginning, set the mood. Create an imaginary musical group and its itinerary—which includes your city. Post flyers in your classroom publicizing the name of the group at least one week before introducing the lesson. This will create funny rumors and a great deal of excitement about the new group. If you are brave, come dressed up in a real "get-up" on the day the assignment is announced. Brainstorm with students to determine important considerations when planning an itinerary for a group and its concert needs.

This is an excellent lesson to use for cooperative learning. Working in groups of four of five, students should create an itinerary that allows the most people in the country to see their musical group. The locations of the concert sites must accommodate thousands of fans. Remind students that fans need to eat and sleep. The plans for the itinerary should include a map of the United States, important geographic features of the areas traveled, as well as important sites in each city that hosts the musical group. Students should calculate the mileage from city to city, length of time traveled, and the best routes to take. Ask each group to write a brief description of one city on the route and explain why it was selected as a tour site.

 **10 Foreign Exchange**

◆ **Objective**   • Relate foreign-made goods to foreign countries

◆ **Materials**   • World map
                    • *Foreign Exchange* reproducible (page 22)

This activity will help students become aware that many of the products they use are made in other countries. Provide students with the reproducible list of countries and companies on page 22. Have students locate the listed nations on a world map. Then review the list of companies and help students identify some of the products that they manufacture. Another possibility is to have students place magazine pictures of the products, product logos, or drawings along the edge of the map and attach them with string to the appropriate nation.

 # Songs across the U.S.A.

⌕ Objective
- Identify locations on a map

⌕ Materials
- United States map
- Blank U.S. (outline) maps
- *U.S. Songs* reproducible (page 23)

For this activity, have students trace a path on a blank U.S. map from state to state as they identify songs written about each state. You'll find a starter list on page 23; challenge students to think of other titles as well. You may wish to have students match up the states with the songs and label the songs on the map. Depending on the age of your class, you may wish to illustrate each label with a symbol such as a musical note. Consider having a sing-a-long using pre-recorded music as students trace the songs from state to state.

Other Geography Activities

These activities focus on other aspects of geography, such as how resources affect settlement, industry, and ways of life.

 # Sing Me a Song

⌕ Objective
- Identify geographic features of an area
- Create a song using geographic information

Invite students to create a song, poem, rap, or advertising jingle about the geographic area (country, state, or area) you are studying in class. Explain that the song must be historically and geographically accurate. Depending on the age group of your students, you might add extra guidelines about the length of the song. Consider performing the song for families or another class.

13 Travel Time Brochures

Objective
- Recognize that geography affects tourism
- Locate sites on a map

Materials
- Construction paper
- Magazines
- Travel brochures

Teacher Tips

Creating travel brochures and itineraries is an effective way for students to discover various places across the United States and around the world. As a teacher, you can shape this activity depending on what you want to accomplish. Students can produce a brochure highlighting a specific area, specific city, state, or country. Have students find the major cities, historical sites, state or national parks, tourist attractions, topography, and vegetation. Students can also write to the State Department of Highways and Public Transportation, or the consulate of a particular country for information. A great teachable moment—letter-writing skills!

Bring in examples of travel brochures. Ask students, "Why would you like to visit these places?" Discuss what makes the brochures interesting and exciting. Then, brainstorm and list on the board things that should be included in a travel brochure such as climate, historical sites, points of interest.

Discuss how having a brochure which looks "appealing" would encourage tourists to visit a location. Assign students to work in groups and select a place that tourists might visit. Students should then do research to find out at least three reasons why this place might attract visitors. When the groups are ready to create their brochures, show them  that one way is to fold a piece of 8½" by 11" construction paper into three sections. Remind students to include enough pertinent information so that anyone reading the brochure can make an informed decision about whether or not to visit the location. Students can illustrate their brochures with drawings or pictures from magazines.

There's a World in Your Closet

◢ **Objective**
- Recognize global interdependence
- Create a chart

◢ **Materials**
- Blank world (outline) maps

The purpose of this activity is to make students aware of how countries of the world are interconnected, using everyday items such as those which students might find in their own closets. Through their discoveries, students will become more aware of global interdependence.

Have students go through the clothing in their closets and drawers, including shoes, T-shirts, jeans, boots, jackets, shirts, dresses, and other items. Instruct students to read the tags or labels to find the places of origin. Students can then list the items, countries of origin, and materials from which the items were made. Have students share their closet information with the class to create a chart. The chart should indicate the number of items from each country. Provide students with a map and have them color and label all the countries they "found" in their closets.

Ask the students what they thought about their clothing before they conducted their survey. What do they think now?

On a selected day, invite students to come to class dressed in at least three articles of clothing that were made in a different country, and present their findings to the class.

Cookie Island

◢ **Objective**
- Describe the physical features of land

◢ **Materials**
- Chocolate chip cookies
- Napkins

Here's a tasty way to help young students expand their geography vocabulary and develop an understanding of geographic features. Begin by giving each student a cookie. Invite students to pretend the cookie is a geographic area, such as an island. Have students work in pairs to examine the chocolate chip cookie for various physical features and describe these to one another using correct geographical vocabulary. For example, students might "identify" bays, gulfs, or mountain ranges on their cookie. Inevitably, you will have a student who will take a bite of the cookie before you have completed giving the instructions. No problem— Cookie Island just had an earthquake!

 16 **Cookie City**

⌒ **Objective**   • Identify factors that influence the size and location of cities

⌒ **Materials**   • Chocolate chip cookies
                   • Napkins

After you have taught basic geography skills, brainstorm reasons why certain areas grow to become cities (landforms, climate, proximity to water). Divide students into small groups and give each student a chocolate chip cookie and a napkin (for easy clean-up). Direct the groups to examine each cookie. Tell them that the cookie represents a state or country of their choice and that the chips represent cities.

Explain that students will examine the location of the "cities" and determine which one(s) would be considered important based on the criteria discussed. Students should consider both advantages and disadvantages of the cities' locations, along with any factors that might have influenced their growth. Encourage students to be as creative and imaginative as possible.

Students can illustrate their city on paper with a descriptive phrase or name. Students can also construct a road map of the city, marking boundaries, major roads, and landmarks, and indicate different types of land use in the city. When all of the cookies have been analyzed, ask the groups to explain to the rest of class the conclusions they drew. Cookies can then be eaten.

17 Cookie Archaeology

⌣ Objective
- Recognize that human activities have an impact on the environment

◖ Materials
- Chocolate chip cookies
- Napkins
- Toothpicks

As an extension of the Cookie City activity, have students imagine that they are archaeologists. Provide each student with a cookie, a napkin, and several toothpicks. Students become archaeologists as they try very carefully to "dig" up ancient artifacts (chocolate chips) and record their "findings" in each section unearthed. Then lead a discussion of the kinds of things a real archaeologist might find. What resources were used to make these items? What else might these finds tell about the people who left them? After the "archaeological dig," students can either discuss or write about their experience.

Foreign Exchange

Sweden: Volvo, Saab

Japan: Toshiba, Sony, Honda

United Kingdom: Cadbury, Keebler, Scripto, Baskin Robbins

Netherlands and the United Kingdom: Lipton, Shell Oil, Pepsodent

Switzerland: Swatch, Libby, Nestle

Norway: Timex

Germany: Volkswagen

U.S. Songs

Hooray for Hollywood

Houston

Arkansas Traveler

My Old Kentucky Home

Carry Me Back to Old Virginia

Sweet Georgia Brown

Yellow Rose of Texas

California Here I Come

I Left My Heart in San Francisco

Chicago!

New York, New York

Galveston

Rocky Mountain High

Erie Canal

Cincinnati, Ohio

Big D

Streets of Laredo

Red River Valley

Oklahoma

Moon Over Miami

Kansas City

By the Time I Get to Phoenix

Georgia On My Mind

I Love New York

Beautiful Ohio

Texas, Our Texas

Missouri Waltz

Back Home Again in Indiana

Way Down Yonder in New Orleans

Pennsylvania Polka

Battle of New Orleans

San Antonio Stroll

Luckenbach, Texas

Only in Miami

Old Folks at Home

Sports Teams

National Basketball Association

Atlanta Hawks	Cleveland Cavaliers
Golden State Warriors	Los Angeles Lakers
New Jersey Nets	Phoenix Suns
San Antonio Spurs	Dallas Mavericks
Boston Celtics	Miami Heat
Houston Rockets	Portland Trail Blazers
New York Knickerbockers	Denver Nuggets
Utah Jazz	Milwaukee Bucks
Charlotte Hornets	Sacramento Kings
Indiana Pacers	Detroit Pistons
Orlando Magic	Minnesota Timberwolves
Washington Bullets	Seattle SuperSonics
Chicago Bulls	Toronto Raptors
Los Angeles Clippers	Vancouver Grizzlies
Philadelphia 76ers	

According to 1996 NBA listings.

National Football League

National Conference

Eastern Division:

Dallas Cowboys

New York Giants

Philadelphia Eagles

Washington Redskins

Phoenix Cardinals

Central Division:

Chicago Bears

Detroit Lions

Green Bay Packers

Tampa Bay Buccaneers

Minnesota Vikings

Western Division:

Atlanta Falcons

New Orleans Saints

Carolina Panthers

San Francisco 49ers

St. Loius Rams

American Conference

Eastern Division:

Buffalo Bills

Indianapolis Colts

Miami Dolphins

New England Patriots

New York Jets

Central Division:

Houston Oilers

Cincinnati Bengals

Baltimore Ravens

Cleveland Browns

Pittsburgh Steelers

Jacksonville Jaguars

Western Division:

San Diego Chargers

Oakland Raiders

Seattle Seahawks

Denver Broncos

Kansas City Chiefs

According to 1996 NFL listings.

Section Two
HISTORY

Too often, historical information is taught through memorized dates and facts. Students will remember historical periods more vividly if they are allowed to feel a part of the time period through research, hands-on activities, simulations, and the use of primary and secondary sources and literature relating to the time period.

Timeline Activities

Since it is an abstract concept, time often causes students difficulty. Timelines are a wonderful way to present visually events, trends, discoveries, or accomplishments during a particular period. History deals with so many different time periods, and timelines provide a convenient way to frame them. Illustrating a timeline helps students remember events in a much clearer manner. Because sequential order is so important in the study of history, you will find timelines an important part of the curriculum. We have provided the following examples to show you some of the different kinds of timelines we've used in the past.

Types of Timelines:

Historical Event Timeline

British History Timeline

1400s
1455 - War of the Roses

1500s
1534 - Act of Supremacy
1558 - Elizabeth becomes Queen of England
1588 - England defeats the Spanish Armada

1600s
1607 - England founds Virginia Colony
1649 - Charles I on trial for treason
1666 - Disastrous fire breaks out in London

1700s
1707 - Act of Union unites England and Scotland
1763 - End of Seven Years' War
1776 - American colonies officially declare independence

1800s
1803 - War breaks out between Britain and France
1812 - Britain and the United States at war
1837 - Victoria becomes Queen of England

War Timeline

American History War Timeline
1776 - American Revolution
1812 - War with Britain
1846 - War with Mexico
1898 - Spanish-American War
1917 - World War I
1941 - World War II
1950 - Korean War
1968 - Viet Nam War
1991 - Persian Gulf War

Graphic Timeline – Mediterranean History

Parthenon Built in Athens
477–432 B.C.

Destruction of Pompeii
A.D. 79

Romulus Augustus Last Roman Emperor
A.D. 475–476

776 B.C.
First Olympic Games

336–332 B.C.
Alexander the Great Builds Empire

A.D. 324
Constantine Reunites Roman Empire

18 Scramble Time

🡒 **Objectives** • Sequence historical time

🡒 **Materials** • Paper bags

You can use this activity as a review for placing events in chronological order. Organize students into pairs. Give each pair a paper bag that you have filled with small pieces of paper labeled with historic events. Do not include any dates. Explain that students need to unscramble the events and place them in proper order. To extend this activity, have students draw a picture to represent each event on the timeline. You might also have students write three facts about each event.

Teacher Tips

- **Studying explorers? Use a ship's log format to record the chain of events.**
- **Ancient Egypt? Use tissue paper as a form of papyrus and hieroglyphics to tell the stories.**
- **Paper towels make great timelines.**
- **Adding machine tape provides for a long timeline.**
- **Paper chain timelines hung around the room or on a bulletin board make a very colorful classroom.**

19 My Time

 Objectives • Sequence personal data

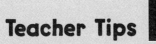 **Materials** • Personal photographs

One of the best ways for students to understand the concept of a timeline is for each student to do one of his or her own life. This is a good way for students to introduce themselves at the beginning of the year. Have students create a timeline of ten important events in their lives.

Teacher Tips

Extend this activity by having students create a parallel timeline showing events happening at the same time in the world.

Encourage students to include events relating to their favorite pastime, hobby, or sport. Suggest that students use actual photographs or drawings that illustrate the events on the timeline.

20 Human Timeline

 **Objectives** • Sequence class data

An entertaining way to introduce timelines is to make a human one. Invite students to line up according to their birth dates, from January 1st to December 31st. To make it more interesting, have students arrange themselves in sequential order through non-verbal communication. That's right...No Talking!

 # Clothesline Timeline

⚒ **Objectives**
- Recognize different time periods
- Sequence historical data

⚒ **Materials**
- Clothesline
- Clothespins

Make a timeline using a clothesline and hang it in the classroom. You can hang it as close to the ceiling as possible, and display it all year. Mark the left end of the timeline with a picture representing where in historical time you will start at the beginning of the school year. For example if you are studying the Jurassic period, you might display a picture of a stegosaurus. As historical events are discussed throughout the year, have students add pictures and dates to represent events. Use clothespins to attach the pictures to your timeline.

 # Pictograph Timeline

⚒ **Objectives**
- Create symbols to represent events
- Sequence personal data

⚒ **Materials**
- Brown paper bags
- Crayons or markers

Pictographs are pictures that tell a story. Some Native American groups recorded the passage of time through pictographs. They used symbols that represented ideas or concepts, not necessarily words. Tanned animal skins, such as deer and buffalo hides, provided a writing surface on which to record important events of a tribe. Have students use pictographs to tell about five major events in their own lives. If possible, provide students with actual symbols that the Native Americans used in their pictographs. Provide students with brown paper bags for their animal hides. Have students crumble and crunch their bag in order to make it soft and pliable, just like a tanned animal hide. Encourage students to devise symbols to tell their story.

Researching and Reporting:
People of the Past

These activities require students to research and report on historical figures from different time periods.

23 Person of the Year

Objectives
- Analyze information about a historical figure
- Develop written communication skills

Materials
- Examples of news/personality-related magazines (*Newsweek, Time, People, Us*)

In this activity, students "become" journalists for a famous news magazine. Their assignment is to select a "Person of the Year" for the next issue. As journalists they need to convince their editor-in-chief that the person they have selected should be given this title. Students write an article clearly stating a position of support for their "Person of the Year." It is important for students to present evidence in support of this person based on research from books, periodicals, and primary and secondary sources. Finally, students should conclude by restating their position and justifying their choice for this prestigious honor. Students can also design a magazine cover honoring this person. Have students give oral presentations, then take a class vote to select the most outstanding person based on criteria the class has selected.

24 Circle Your People

Objectives
- Analyze the interrelationships of historical figures

Have students create a page of circles, placing the name of the historical figure whose life they have researched in the center circle. In the other circles, students place the names of individuals who have been influential in that person's life and explain the importance of these individuals to the central figure.

25 Interview Program

⬥ **Objectives** • Develop written and oral communication skills

Have students write a list of sample interview questions that they might ask a historical figure. Students can work in pairs to do research and role-play an interview of famous people for the class.

26 People Poems

⬥ **Objectives** • Develop written communication skills

This is a great activity for integrating English into the social studies classroom. Students can write a poem about a person they have researched. The poem can be in the form of an acrostic, in which the first letter of each line begins with a letter of the person's name. The lines consist of words or phrases describing the person's characteristics.

> **Example of an Acrostic:**
>
> **L** anky
> **I** ntelligent
> **N** ote-worthy
> **C** ivil War President
> **O** ral communicator
> **L** awyer by profession
> **N** ick-named "Honest Abe."

Another type of poem is the diamante, which takes its name from the diamond-shaped form it makes. In order for students to make a diamante, they need to follow the line-by-line formula on page 33.

person's first name
two adjectives that describe the person
three "ing" words related to the subject
four nouns that describe the person
three verbs that tell how the person acted or felt
two adjectives that describe the person
person's last name

Example of Diamante:

Abraham
lanky, bearded
thinking, caring, feeling
emancipator, leader, president, martyr
commanded, led, assassinated
honest, presidential
Lincoln

27 Poster People

⚑ **Objectives** • Analyze information about a historical figure

◥ **Materials** • Art supplies

In this activity students make a poster to honor a person who has, through time (past or present) made a significant contribution to history. The posters should advertise the person's life and accomplishments. Students might also include quotes from the person on their poster.

28 What's in the News?

⚑ **Objectives** • Analyze information about a historical figure
• Develop written communication skills

◥ **Materials** • Current magazines

Divide the class into small groups and explain that each group will make its own "Person of the Year" magazine. All the articles must be about one person and the time period in which he or she lived. You might have students bring in current magazines and discuss the types of articles and advertisements found in them. Have students brainstorm ideas for their magazine and then write their comments on the board.

"Person of the Year" Magazine

Students might include the following:
- pictures/drawings about the person's life
- an editorial on why this person should be named "Person of the Year"
- what others have said about the person
- timeline of important events and accomplishments
- advertisement from that time period
- political cartoons
- other important events of the time period

 **29 People from the Past**

◁ **Objectives**
- Recognize important historical figures and their contributions
- Develop oral communication skills

Begin the lesson by asking, "Have you ever met anyone famous?" This question may generate a variety of responses from students and is a perfect lead-in for the activity. Then

ask, "What do you think you would ask a famous historical person if he or she walked into the room?" Write students' responses on the blackboard. Model by playing the role of one important person and let students ask you questions. Then provide a list of people for students to research. If possible, have each student select a different historical figure, and write a short report about that person. Provide research materials in the classroom or arrange for library time. On the day of the activity, ask students to come to class dressed up as their figure. The idea is to take on the persona of that figure through a combination of dress, make-up, props, or speech. Students can question each other in order to discover the identities of the "people from the past" who have come to visit their classroom.

30 Convincing Collages

Objectives
- Develop effective use of persuasive writing skills

Materials
- Art supplies
- Old magazines and catalogs
- Scissors
- Glue

After the students have researched their historical figure, have them present their findings to the class by creating a "Convincing Collage." Each student creates a collage consisting of 3-5 words/phrases and 3-5 pictures/drawings representing the person and their achievements. The design of the collage should in some way symbolize the person and the time period in which he or she lived.

31 Adults Were Young Once, Too!

Objectives
- Relate past to present
- Identify and explain the characteristics of primary and secondary sources
- Identify major cultural changes in the past decades

Materials
- Prepared questionnaire

Start the lesson with a statement such as: "My mother told me that when she was young she walked two miles, up hill, in the ice and snow, to get to school every day." Several students will usually tell you that their parents do the same thing. This is a wonderful lead-in for a discussion about how things have changed. For example, tell students about the first time you saw a color TV program or used a microwave oven. The example you use should be something that your students take for granted but was not available when you were their age. Formulate questions with students about things they would like to find out from older people. Discuss primary and secondary sources and their importance. After you have collected students' questions, create a questionnaire based on their interest.

Give each student a prepared questionnaire with the questions they helped to develop. Their mission is to seek out and interview the oldest people they can find about the changes that have taken place during their lifetime. At the top of each questionnaire, put a list of questions that can be answered with "yes" or "no." Follow these with students' questions. A sample questionnaire is below.

Teacher Tips

This activity can be expanded in many directions, both oral and written.

- **Create an interview poster with illustrations, pictures, snapshots, and other memorabilia.**
- **Have students write a paper on their discoveries.**
- **Videotape an interview with a senior citizen to record history for posterity. This is especially meaningful if the senior is a family member.**
- **After gathering all the information, have students either write a story using the data or present their findings orally to the class.**

Were you born before the use of...

Penicillin?
Hula hoops?
Plastic?
Frozen food?
Ball-point pens?
Instant coffee?

Copy machines?
Polio vaccine?
Credit cards?
Contact lenses?
Dishwashers?
Low-fat diets?

Questions:

What was it like when you were my age?
What did you do for fun?
What was a popular fad?
Were there any fast-food restaurants?
How much did a soft drink and pizza cost?
What was a popular song?
What type of clothes did you wear to school?
How did you live without a TV, computer,
     answering machine, blow dryer, CD player?
Did you have a curfew?
Did you really walk to school two miles uphill everyday?

 **Family Crest**

 **Objectives** • Associate historical figures with particular events

Materials • Art supplies

Students can create a family crest for the person whose life they have researched. They might use symbols to illustrate the important events or influences in the person's life.

 **Summit Conference**

Objectives • Analyze information about a historical figure
• Recognize different points of view

Follow the instructions for the "People from the Past" activity, but tell students to be prepared to meet other famous people who lived during the same period. Hold a classroom summit conference so that students can present the ideas and viewpoints from their personality's perspective.

 **Multicultural People**

Objectives • Reinforce multicultural appreciation

Have each student research an important person from his or her cultural heritage. Students should prepare to give an oral report on the highlights of this person's life and the contributions he or she made to the culture. Students might dress as the person they represent.

35 Paper Plate People

Objectives
- Identify key facts about a historical person or event

Materials
- Paper plates (plastic and foam plates will not work)
- Tongue depressors
- Crayons or markers

Have students research a famous person from the era being studied in class. Once they have completed the research, students draw symbols that characterize that individual's contribution to society, along with a profile or portrait of the person, on a paper plate. On the back of the plate, students list three clues that they can read aloud as the rest of the class tries to identify the person. The tongue depressor can be attached to the back of the paper plate in order for the student to handle the plate more easily.

Teacher Tips

- **Group students by time periods and have them create a short skit using their paper plate people. Students can perform the skit for the rest of the class.**
- **Have students create a "paper plate people" timeline by holding their "people" and lining up in chronological order.**
- **Pair students and have them interview each other and then introduce one another's personalities to the class.**
- **Have students write a short paragraph about their paper plate person.**
- **Create a bulletin board display using the paper plate people. Title it "Faces in History."**

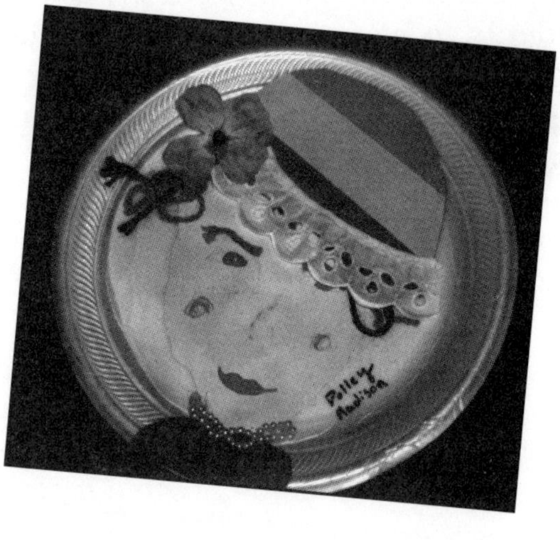

36 Group Collages

 **Objectives**
- Identifying a point of view

Materials
- Art supplies
- Old magazines and catalogs
- Glue
- Scissors

Divide the class into small groups according to topics. For example, if you are studying the Civil War, divide the class into Confederates and Unionists. Have the groups brainstorm a list of people, places, achievements, and events. Using this list, students can then create a collage using at least ten words or phrases and pictures or drawings symbolizing their topic. Each group then explains its collage to the class. The collages are also an excellent way to review for a test.

37 Resumes, Resumes, Resumes

Objectives
- Summarize information about a historical figure

Materials
- Resumes

Today, in order to apply for most jobs, it's necessary to have a resume. This document uses clear and concise language to state a person's accomplishments and background. Successful resumes demonstrate that the jobseeker has the right experience and education for a position and show a clear sense of career purpose. In this activity, students will write a resume for a historical figure.

Teacher Tips

Pair students and have them take turns playing interviewer and interviewee as they take on the persona of the figure they researched and interview for a job.

Begin by having students brainstorm what they think a resume should include. Some possibilities are work experience, volunteer experience, skills, awards and honors, activities, education, special training, and military experience. Have on hand examples of real resumes for students to examine and use as models.

Bind the completed resumes together for a class book to be kept in the room for future reference.

38 Hall of History

◢ **Objectives**
- Recognize the contributions of people in history
- Synthesize information

◣ **Materials**
- Large sheets of butcher paper
- Paints and brushes
- Crayons and markers

Organize students into pairs or small groups to research a famous person. After completing sufficient research, students create a "life-size" figure. Supply each group with a large piece of butcher paper. Students then trace one member of the group to create a life-size image. Students should create characteristics and clothing to portray their person accurately.

Teacher Tips

This is a wonderful activity to do during Black History Month, or at any time when you are emphasizing a particular group. There's no need to limit this activity to just historical figures: your class can create a Hall of Heroes, Hall of Presidents, Hall of Poets, or any other hall that you wish.

Have students synthesize information about the person and write five facts they consider the most important about this individual and his or her accomplishments. Students should write these facts around the body they've created, then present their "person" to the class. Display the finished figures in the classroom or in the hall. As successive periods of history are covered, you can add other figures to the "gallery."

39 Business Cards

⚑ **Objectives**
- Evaluate information about a historical figure
- Summarize a person's contribution to history

⚑ **Materials**
- Business cards
- 5" x 7" index cards

In this activity students research a historical figure, evaluate the most important facts about that person, and then put those facts on a business card. Students can also come up with a slogan that summarizes this person's achievements. A few days before you plan on doing this activity, ask students to collect as many business cards as they can and bring them to class. Encourage students to explain the kinds of information they can discover from the cards. Write this information on the board.

Teacher Tips

Adapt this activity for the first week of school by having students create their own business card. They might include information such as: favorite hobbies, pastimes, school subjects, or any other facts that might help you to to get to know them. Laminate the cards so students can keep them throughout the year.

Business Card Information:

Name of person	Occupation or career
Name of company	Address, telephone number, fax number
E-mail address	Why you need their services

Logo or slogan – you might want to list some different slogans on the board so students will have a better idea of why a catchy slogan is important.

Before students begin to work, remind them that they will have to adapt a contemporary business card to one for a historical figure. For example, George Washington would not have a telephone number, fax number, or e-mail address.

40 Report Cards

⌔ **Objectives**
- Recognize historical figures and their contributions
- Evaluate information about a historical figure

◔ **Materials**
- Construction paper

Have students select a person to research on their own or from a list you provide. Inform students that they are going to design a "report card" for this person. Ask students to consider how they would rate this person and how this person compares to other people of his or her period. Have students create a report card using standard grades (A,B,C,D, or F) in at least five categories. Here is a list of suggestions:

- leadership skills
- organization and planning
- community relations
- perseverance
- ethical conduct
- intelligence
- personal qualities
- fulfillment of expectations
- decision-making skills
- treatment of others
- professionalism
- responsiveness to suggestions
- contributions to history

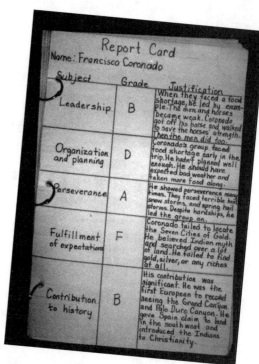

Next to each grade, have students justify the mark with a two or three sentence explanation. Students may give any grade as long as it is justified by specific facts and examples.

Focusing on Events and Ideas

The events of the past lead to those of the present and future. In these activities students will look at some of those past events.

41  High Tech

Objectives
- Analyze events of the past
- Identify cultural changes over time

Materials
- poster paper
- colored markers

The Industrial Revolution was a turning point in the history of mankind. The advent of machinery not only changed the way work was done, but completely changed the way people lived, including the creation of a middle class. The rate of technological and cultural change in the twentieth century has increased the degrees of difference between the lifestyles of preceding generations.

Have a class discussion about the "good old days." (First specify which historical era you consider this bygone period to be.) Ask students what they think life would be like without items such a remote control, blow dryer, or computer. If available, you may want to show a film clip of life in the late 1800s, for example, *Little House on the Prairie*. Then have students work in groups to make "Then and Now" charts on poster paper. For each contemporary device that students list under the "Now" column, they should write in the "Then" column what people used to achieve a similar result before the device in question was invented.

Teacher Tips

Ask students whether people have to "reinvent the wheel" every time they want to do something new. Discuss how various inventors only improved upon earlier items. Stress that the wheel and plow are also examples of technology and as significant to their time period as computers are today. Spur discussion with questions such as:
- **What technological devices do you use every day?**
- **What kinds of problems have been caused by technology? (Emotional and physical stress, man replaced by machine, pollution.)**
- **What technology would you predict for 20 years from now? 50 years? 100 years?**

◒ **Objectives**
- Identify historical events
- Develop written communication skills

◒ **Materials**
- Art supplies

Young children learn basic sounds and information from readers and ABC books. Creating historical "ABC" books is a remarkable teaching tool for understanding various time periods. It can be used with any area of study. Students can design an ABC book that is similar to the children's books they used to learn the alphabet. Students may work individually or with partners. To remind students of what an ABC book should contain, you might hand out an instruction sheet such as the one on this page related to the Revolutionary War. After the books are completed, have students share them with lower grade classes.

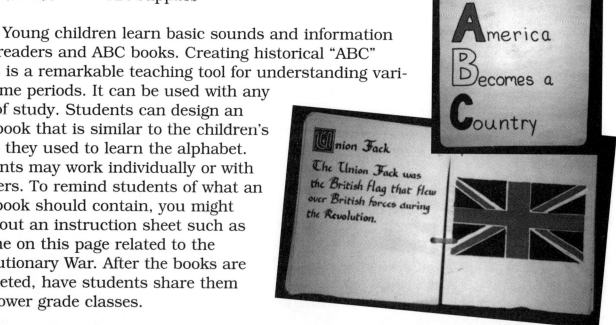

American Revolution - ABC Book Instructions

Your book should contain the following:
- A decorated cover with the name(s) of you as the author(s).
- Each letter of the alphabet on a separate page.
- A word or term relating to the Revolutionary War for each letter.
- A thorough definition or explanation of each word written in terms that a younger child could understand.
- An illustration for each word. Illustrations can be drawn, traced, copied, cut from magazines or newspapers, or done on the computer.
- Be consistent throughout your book. Make it as much like a real ABC book as possible. Your grade will be determined by craftsmanship, creativity, thoroughness, and neatness.
- Remember that spelling and grammar count.

43 Lights, Camera, Action!

⌂ **Objectives**
- Identify and analyze events in history
- Develop communication skills

⌂ **Materials**
- Construction paper
- Colored markers or crayons
- Magazine pictures or drawings
- Cardboard box
- Two wooden dowels (length will depend on size of box)

In this activity, students make a 10-frame film-strip about a historical event. Organize students into pairs or small groups and have them select an event in history as their topic. Students should work together to plan and organize the information and visuals that they will use for each frame. Remind them that a frame may include pictures, diagrams, maps, cartoons, tables, or graphs. On the bottom of each frame, students need to write a short caption. In addition to the frames, they should plan a narrative to accompany the filmstrip. Students might record their narrative and include appropriate background music. Suggest that they include a signal (beep) to mark the beginning of each frame.

44 Songs of War and Peace

⌂ **Objectives**
- Analyze the meaning of a song

⌂ **Materials**
- Songbooks

Throughout time, people have used song in a variety of ways. Historians often study the lyrics of songs to help them interpret the historical events of an era. Songs often make statements or tell a story about a time period.

Find at least three songs written about a particular time period in history. For example:

Civil War: "When Johnny Comes Marching Home" and "Dixie"
American Revolution: "Yankee Doodle Dandy" and "Revolutionary Tea"
Viet Nam: "Where Have All the Flowers Gone?" and "Blowin' in the Wind"

Have students listen carefully to the lyrics and reflect on the thoughts and feelings of the people during the period represented. Encourage students to then develop and write questions about this time period. They might also draw a picture or mural to illustrate what the song is saying.

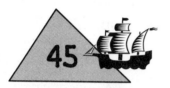

45 Footprints through History

⚐ **Objectives**
- Recognize cause-effect relationships between people and events

⚐ **Materials**
- Scissors
- Colored construction paper

In this activity students trace the thoughts and actions of a person as they relate to a historical event. For example, they might focus on the role of Thomas Jefferson in the birth of this nation. Assign each student a historical figure to investigate for a specific event. Students should concentrate on how this person influenced the event. After completing their research, have students trace one of their feet. They should make enough copies of the footprint for each fact that they plan to write. After the footprints are finished, laminate them and display them on a bulletin board.

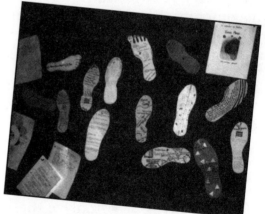

Don't limit yourself to footprints. You can also use outlines of buildings or other symbols for historical information.

 # Explorer's Notebook

Objectives
• Synthesize historical information
• Interpret primary and secondary sources

Materials
• Art supplies

Divide the students into groups of three or four. Assume the role of a European monarch in the Age of Exploration and provide each group, or "crew," with the necessary provisions for a journey to the New World. Tell students that they will have certain requirements (see suggestions on the next page) to meet if they expect to be rewarded for their achievements. In order for students to fulfill their contract, they must complete the voyage and return with evidence of their findings in the new land. For this activity, gathering evidence will be a matter of research and creativity. Books, maps, diaries, and other sources of primary and secondary materials should be used. When they have "returned from their journey" and are ready, students should present themselves before you, the monarch, and detail their findings. You may wish to award compensation for these findings.

Create an "Explorer's Notebook" for your journey

It should include:
• A public announcement alerting people to the voyage.
• A "want ad" to help attract crew members.
• A map tracing the voyage from the sponsoring country to the New World and back.
• Information about your crew, ship(s), problems faced, and weather.
• Specific information about the area(s) you "explored." This should include items such as plants, animals, minerals, agriculture, and human life. You may also want to include drawings you made while exploring.
• A letter to the monarch drawing conclusions about the voyage and persuading him or her to either continue or abandon similar explorations in the future.

47 Hula Hoopla

◁ **Objectives**
- Classify and organize data
- Compare and contrast different ideas, points of view, or events

◁ **Materials**
- Index cards
- Two hula hoops

A Venn Diagram (named after John Venn, an English logician) is a wonderful technique to help children represent logical relations in a visual manner. With such a strong emphasis on individual learning styles, what better way to help a visual learner understand abstract concepts than hula hoops in the classroom! Students love the idea, no matter if they are in kindergarten or high school and hula hoops provide "awesome" circles, much better than circles drawn on the chalkboard.

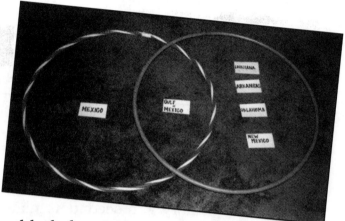

Teacher Tips

After you have completed the hula hoop activity, follow up with a writing assignment on the topic. Ask students how they would organize their essays. Help them see that in completing the Venn diagram, they have actually placed related events or ideas into groups and established an organization which can be translated into a "compare and contrast" essay.

Place two hula hoops on either the floor or blackboard, making sure they overlap, forming a center section. Label each section of the diagram to show what is being compared. Have students write facts about two events, points of view, or people on index cards. Place the cards in a pile, then have students take turns picking a card and deciding which part of the Venn diagram it belongs in. Use the completed diagram to compare and contrast the event.

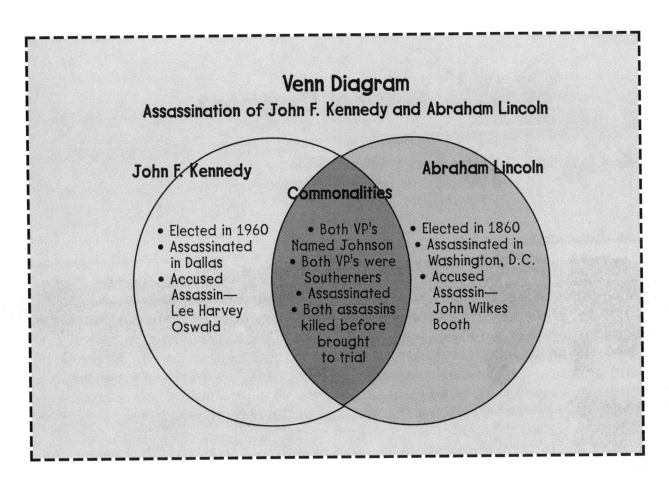

Venn Diagram
Assassination of John F. Kennedy and Abraham Lincoln

John F. Kennedy

- Elected in 1960
- Assassinated in Dallas
- Accused Assassin— Lee Harvey Oswald

Commonalities

- Both VP's Named Johnson
- Both VP's were Southerners
- Assassinated
- Both assassins killed before brought to trial

Abraham Lincoln

- Elected in 1860
- Assassinated in Washington, D.C.
- Accused Assassin— John Wilkes Booth

48 Cartoon Notebook

◁ **Objectives**
- Interpret political cartoons

◁ **Materials**
- Political cartoons
- Art supplies

Have students create a political cartoon notebook. The notebook should include 10-15 political or social satire cartoons. Provide the students with a short list of questions to answer about each cartoon. For example:

- What is the main idea of the cartoon?
- What is the particular issue, problem or news story?
- What is the cartoonist's point of view? Do you feel that it was communicated?

Teacher Tips

- To get students started on political cartoons, make copies of recent cartoons from the local newspaper. Delete the original caption and have students make up their own.
- Have students make up an original cartoon strip about an event in history.

49 Political Cartoons

Objectives
- Interpret a political cartoon
- Distinguish fact from opinion
- Establish a point of view

Materials
- Current political cartoons
- Art supplies

About a week before you plan to do this lesson, check the newspapers and magazines for current cartoons. If you discuss current events in your class, try and get a cartoon about something you have been discussing. Point out that through the use of political cartoons, the artist attempts to inform the public and to arouse and influence readers. Begin by using an overhead projector to show the class a current political cartoon you've copied onto a transparency. Ask students what they think the message of the cartoon is.

Discuss with students the concept of satire—a technique that pokes fun at people, ideas, and institutions. This is accomplished because satire focuses on such things as mistakes, weaknesses, foolishness, and immorality. Satire is used to raise questions about current trends and events or political issues. Satire can be gentle and sympathetic or bitter and angry.

Discuss with students the purposes of a political cartoon, and write their ideas on the board. Also discuss with students the idea of caricature drawing, and how it is used. (A caricature is a drawing where the most outstanding features are exaggerated to create a humorous effect.) Cartoons of political and social satire are simple graphic presentations (drawings) of opinion. What makes them so effective is that through the use of humor, the artist conveys a serious message that causes the reader to focus on an issue.

Once the importance and significance of cartoons have been established, it's time for students to become cartoonists, too. Of course, you'll have a student tell you that he or she can't draw. Not a problem... show students some famous cartoon characters that are simple line drawings. This is not as difficult as it seems since most cartoons are simple line drawings.

Have your students select a main idea for their cartoon. The main idea is a single, clear point about a newsworthy issue. As the cartoonist, the student will need to express a point of view.

50 Roadside Historical Markers

Objectives
- Identify events that happened at a particular place
- Explain significance of a historical marker

Materials
- Construction paper
- Crayons or markers
- Pictures of historical markers

To begin this lesson, students must have a good idea of what a historical marker is. It is important to have students contribute as much information as possible. Ask: What is the purpose of a historical marker? Have students ever stopped along the highway to read a historical marker? Have they ever been to a historical site such as the Alamo or Gettysburg? How are historical markers worded? (Examples: "Here was fought...," "This site was...," "At this exact spot...," "Here lies...," "...slept here.")

Tell students to pretend that they have been asked to create a historical marker for a site in their community. It could be one that already exists or one of their choosing. Students may need to do preliminary research to decide on the site. If the site already has a marker, then the one students create must be different. Ask the five W's... who...what... when...where...why.

It is important for students to realize that historical markers are seen by thousands of people, and therefore must be easy to read and include all the pertinent information. Students should try to make their markers interesting and visually appealing.

Teacher Tips

- Give this assignment to students when they go out of town, visit grandparents, or to complete during a school holiday.
- If your city has an interesting history, create a bulletin board with historical markers. Assign a different place for each student to investigate and then place these on a map of the city.
- Make a guidebook to historical markers in your city.
- Keep this activity in a classroom folder for students who are always asking for "extra credit" assignments.

 **51** Signs of the Times

 Objectives
• Analyze information about a historical period
• Develop both written and non-verbal communication skills
• Evaluate and synthesize information

One of the best ways to analyze an era of history is to recognize the slogans of the times. Often these slogans were publicly displayed, and many times consisted of only a few words or sentences. These slogans ran the gamut from the inspirational to critiques of daily life.

After students have researched a particular time period, they will be able to develop a plausible creative "sign of the time." Write some slogans of various times on the board, for example, "Let them eat cake," "Give me liberty or give me death," and "Make my day!" Brainstorm other slogans with the class and write responses on the board. Have students create their own slogans from the historical period they have just studied. Since these slogans are frequently chosen as the subjects of commercials, T-shirts, bumper stickers, wall plaques, and certificates, your students will have a variety of ways to display their "signs of the times."

Teacher Tips

Many words used today were once slang or part of a slogan of a particular time period. With each historical period new words and expressions spring into existence. Most often, people use these words without any idea of where they came from. Discovering the words from a particular era is a good activity to integrate English into a social studies classroom.

Section Three
CULTURE

In this ever-growing, multicultural world, students need to develop an appreciation of their own culture and an understanding of other cultures and their contributions to history. Sharing foods, holidays, and customs can help develop multicultural awareness among all of our students.

Art Activities

Students can both express what they have learned through art and acquire information about the past through art.

52. How I See It

⚫ **Objectives** • Evaluate visual evidence

🔺 **Materials** • Old photographs

This activity can easily integrate Social Studies with Language Arts and Reading. Provide students with copies of early photographs and have them select one each and write about what the photograph means to them. Ask students to discuss how the picture reflects the lifestyle of the people portrayed. Students might follow up by writing a creative story about the picture.

53. Portrait of the Times

⚫ **Objectives** • Understand the relationship between art and history
• Identify ways in which art is used to convey important historical ideas

🔺 **Materials** • Pictures of paintings
• Art Supplies

Have students create their own artistic portrayal of the times. They can use information that they have learned in class to depict the lifestyle of the people they are studying. Remind them that, "A picture is worth a thousand words." The picture should be reflective of the historical time period.

 **54 Totem Tales**

Objectives
- Understand facets of Native American cultures
- Interpret the art of Native American groups of the Pacific Northwest

Materials
- Cereal boxes, oatmeal containers, ice cream tubs, rug rollers, wood, appliance boxes, etc.
- Pictures of actual totem poles
- Paints, crayons, markers

Throughout history, people have left many different kinds of records. Some Native American tribes of the Pacific Northwest created totem poles to record their family histories symbolically. Poles were decorated with animals or faces that represented the history of the families who made them. These intricately carved and brilliantly painted totems told a story. The artist sometimes took years to complete a totem. Many tribes carved special emblems on the poles to show who had created them. Today, few totems are being made, but many of those made years ago are still standing.

Have students create a totem pole, in three parts, that tells the story of their own past, present, and future. Students can construct their totems from cereal boxes, oatmeal containers, wood, or other materials. Before beginning, they should decide what they wish to chronicle about their past, present, and future. Suggest that they use animal features or characteristics to represent qualities they possess or demonstrate.

Note: Totem poles are read from the top to the bottom.

55 A Good Look

Objectives
- Understand the relationship between art and history
- Evaluate visual evidence

Materials
- Reproductions of paintings that tell a story

Write the saying, "A picture is worth a thousand words" on the board. Ask students what this means; write their responses on the board. Then display a reproduction of a painting that relates to the period of history the class is studying. If you are studying Native Americans in the 1800s, for example, show a painting by George Catlin or Frederick Remington (or show slides of these paintings). Ask students to examine the art to learn about how Native Americans lived in the past. Tell students to look for clues that suggest culture or environment. For example, if you show a picture of George Catlin's "Buffalo Chase," you can lead the students into a discussion of the importance of the buffalo to the people of the plains. Photographs work as well as paintings. Many students are visual learners, and these activites are wonderful ways for them to be successful. Art has always been an exciting means of communication.

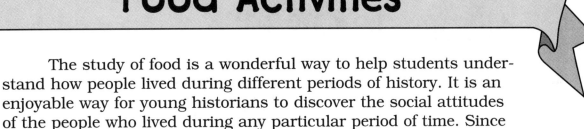

Food Activities

The study of food is a wonderful way to help students understand how people lived during different periods of history. It is an enjoyable way for young historians to discover the social attitudes of the people who lived during any particular period of time. Since food plays such a significant role in all of our lives, we have included a food section, a "smorgasbord" of ideas.

56 Food Collage

◁ **Objectives** • Identify characteristics of other cultures

◁ **Materials** • Old magazines and catalogs
• Art supplies

With partners, have students find pictures of different foods representing a variety of ethnic backgrounds. After the pictures have been collected, students can make a collage to be shared with the class.

57 Recipe Ready

◁ **Objectives** • Share cultural heritage
• Locate places on a map

◁ **Materials** • Recipes
• Art supplies

Ask students to bring to class a sample of a dish that represents their individual ethnicity. Each student should also bring a copy of the recipe so that the class can make a collected recipe book. Students can show on a world map the countries which represent their cultural background, as well as share any other interesting facts about the culture.

58 How We Eat

⬤ **Objectives** • Identify characteristics and customs of different cultural groups

Share with your students the following information about how meals are eaten in other countries. See what additional information your students can add or how many of them have eaten some of these dishes. Perhaps a field trip to an ethnic restaurant could be scheduled or examples of some of these foods might be brought into class and shared.

Eating habits from around the world ...

- In most Latin American countries, the main meal is eaten in the middle of the day. In Brazil, lunch might be boiled rice and mashed black beans, tomato salad, and a chicken dish. Water with a little lime juice added is a common drink. Most people eat special corn pancakes called "tortillas" that may contain one of a variety of fillings.
- In China, a family might eat steamed rice or noodles with vegetables, eggs, or fish. Sometimes a soya-bean sauce is added.
- In Greece, a lunch or dinner might include cheese, bread, olives, fruit, and meat-kabobs on a skewer.
- Boiled rice, vegetables, and fresh fruit are major parts of the Japanese diet. Fish is either lightly fried, stewed, or raw. Prepared raw fish is called sushi.
- Russians typically eat dark rye bread, boiled potatoes, and vegetable soup.
- A Tunisian family might have a bowl of couscous and boiled ground wheat eaten with a vegetable or meat sauce.

 ## Corn Flat Cakes

Objectives • Experience customs of different cultural groups

Materials • Shelled dried corn
• Grinding tool (e.g., mortar and pestle)

Maize was first cultivated over 7,000 years ago. Maize became a versatile source of food eaten in a variety of ways. After its introduction into this country, maize was eaten in much the same way as it is today, boiled, roasted, or ground. Some Native American groups ground the maize into flour, and mixed it with water to form flat cakes of bread. Others boiled the flour in water, making a thick soup.

Bring in (or if possible have students bring in) shelled dried corn (available at feed stores) and a grinding tool. Have students grind the corn into powder, mix with water, and bake. Remember, Native American women did all this by hand, in addition to planting, tending, and harvesting the corn!

 ## Cultural Food-Fest

Objectives • Identify characteristics of different cultural groups

Materials • Paper plates
• Plastic tableware
• Napkins
• Tablecloths
• Placecards for names and origins of dishes

This activity helps promote cultural awareness among students and reinforces the idea of the United States as a "salad bowl," in which everyone's culture contributes to the "flavor" of the whole country. Have students ask their parents and grandparents to supply recipes that represent their ethnic group. Students will also need to ask their family why this recipe is special to their heritage so they can share this information with the class. Ask students to prepare their recipe at home to bring to school. On the day of the "Food-Fest," present the dishes by organizing them according to ethnic groups, or whether they are main dishes, appetizers, desserts, etc. As students sample the foods, they can tell each other about their special family recipes.

61 Foods from around the World

Objectives • Recognize that cultures often borrow from one another

Americans have borrowed many foods from other cultures. Ask students where the food items listed below originated. Have students list other foods of foreign origin, for example: croissants (crescent rolls); crepes (blintzes).

Foreign Foods

1. oatmeal
2. olives
3. hot dogs
4. flan
5. teriyaki
6. spaghetti
7. mayonnaise
8. pizza
9. gingerbread
10. baklava
11. crepes
12. black-eyed peas
13. egg rolls
14. coleslaw
15. beef stroganoff
16. sandwich
17. chorizo
18. chili

Answers: 1. Scotland 2. Greece, Italy, Spain 3. Germany 4. Spain 5. Japan 6. China 7. France 8. Italy, 9 Sweden and Germany 10. Greece 11. France 12. Africa 13. China 14. Russia 15. Russia 16. England 17. Mexico 18. Mexico

Teacher Tips

- **Once students have discovered where these foods originated, have them locate the countries on a world map.**
- **Have students take this list to the grocery store. Ask them to list the items they can find, the cost of each item, and the section of the store in which it is found. Discuss with students why some found more items than their classmates and whether the stores' locations had any effect on the types of items found.**

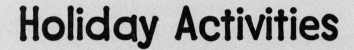

Holiday Activities

Celebrating holidays is an exciting way to investigate different cultures and develop map skills at the same time. Countries all over the world have national holidays. Although many holidays may have originated as a national celebration in one country, they have since spread to other countries. The celebration of holidays can effectively be used to stimulate a variety of class activities.

62 Origin of Holidays

Objectives
- Identify different cultural groups by their holidays
- Understand the influence other cultures have on our lives

Materials
- *Holidays around the World* reproducible (page 63)
- World map

Have students research the origin of different holidays and how they are celebrated in that country. If a holiday is also celebrated in the United States, does it have the same meaning? Are the celebrations similar? Once the students have shared the information about the holiday, they can then locate its country of origin on a map.

63 Holiday Scrapbook

Objectives
- Learn how holidays are celebrated in other cultures

Materials
- Art supplies

Have students choose a holiday from another culture to research. After they present their holiday information to class orally, have students create an illustrated written page about the holiday. Make a large class scrapbook with each student's contribution. Keep the holiday scrapbook in the classroom.

Latitude and Longitude of Holidays

Objectives • Locate places on a map

Materials • *Holidays around the World* reproducible (page 63)
• World Map

For older students, use the information on the reproducible to play a game. Call out a holiday and give clues to its location by latitude and longitude. For example, *Cinco de Mayo* is celebrated at 20 degrees N. latitude, 100 degrees W. longitude. Where is this? Have students consult maps to determine the answer.

Holiday Calendar

Objectives • Learn how holidays are celebrated in other cultures and countries

Materials • Art supplies

Have students work in groups to learn about holidays in other countries. You might assign a month to each group. Have each group fill out a calendar with the holidays it found. Then create a class calendar from students' research. Celebrate some of the holidays with traditional observances during the year.

Holidays Around the World

Aloha Festival	Hawaii	October - November
Beach Day	Uruguay	December 8
Bastille Day	France	July 14
Bolshevik Uprising	Moscow	November 7
Boxing Day	England	December 26
Carnevale	Italy	Beginning of Lent
Children's Day	Japan	June 6
Cinco de Mayo	Mexico City	May 5
Dominion Day	Canada	July 1
Israel Independence Day	Israel	May 14
Independence Day	United States	July 4
Kalevala Day	Finland	February 28
Mardi Gras	United States	Beginning of Lent
Oktoberfest	Germany	October 17
Salzburg Festival	Austria	Summer
St. Patrick's Day	Ireland	March 17
Texas Independence Day	Texas	March 21
Chinese New Year	China	Date varies (usually late January)

FRANKLIN PIERCE COLLEGE LIBRARY

00103022

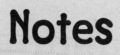

Notes